Going Home:

A Companion Guide for Foster Children

By

Heather J. Cuthbertson

ISBN: 0-9845801-1-5
ISBN-13: 978-0-9845801-1-8
Library of Congress Control Number: 2011902120

First Published by *AuthorMike Ink*, 05/15/2012

www.AuthorMikeInk.com

AuthorMike Ink and its logo are trademarked by *AuthorMike Ink*.

Printed in the United States of America

Going Home:

A Companion Guide for

Foster Children

By

Heather J. Cuthbertson

Part I

What's Happening?

Foster care is not where bad kids go. It is not a punishment. You didn't do anything wrong. It's the truth. Say it out loud whenever you'd like. In fact, you are special—yes, *you*!

You are so special that this book was made just for you, and you can do whatever you want with it while you learn about foster care. You can color. Write. Scribble. Go ahead. No one will stop you.

All you have to do is turn the page.

Chapter 1

"But This Isn't My Home..."

Entering and Living in Foster Care

I bet you have a hundred questions racing around your mind about foster care, like what *is* foster care? Who are foster parents? And why do you have to live in a foster home? But first, it is important to know that foster care is all about you.

What?!

Foster care is for kids, like you, who need grown-ups to care for them. All kids need grown-ups to make them dinner, wash their clothes, make sure they brush their teeth, and, most importantly, give them love.

But when grown-ups become sick, go to jail, or have problems that make it hard for them to take care of their children, kids go to foster care so that other adults can take care of them.

Entering foster care can be hard or easy. Every kid is different and feels different things—you are no exception. No matter how you feel, you need to know that sometimes it's better to allow other grown-ups to take care for you. That way, you can simply be a kid and worry about kid things.

FOSTER PARENTS are grown-ups who take care of children when their parents cannot. Foster parents do not come to your home. Instead, you go to their home. This is called a FOSTER HOME because it's your foster parent's house.

Not all foster homes are alike.

Sometimes foster homes have both a foster mom and a foster dad. Or there may be one foster mom or one foster dad. Other kids might also live in your foster home. They are called your FOSTER BROTHERS and FOSTER SISTERS.

Like most parents, foster parents have rules kids need to follow. These rules keep everyone safe. If you follow your foster parent's rules, then you get to do fun things like spend the night with friends or stay up later on Friday night. Make sure to ask your foster parents what sort of privileges they allow.

Will I ever have to move to another foster home?

It does happen, but for good reasons.

One reason might be that another foster home can take you and your siblings (if you have any) together. Or your foster home is not a good fit because it's too far away from your school or you don't get along with your foster siblings. Another reason could be that you don't feel safe. If you *ever* feel unsafe, you must tell somebody right away.

Everyone wants to make sure you are happy in your foster home. Because, don't forget, foster care is all about you!

Chapter 1 Workbook

Today is (date): _____.

My name is_____ and this is my foster care book.

I am _____ years old.

My birthday is _____ and, next year, I'll be

_____ years old.

My parents' names:

_____.

I have a: (circle)   brother   sister

My brother's and/or sister's name(s):

_____.

The school I attend is named

_____.

I am in the _____ grade.

My favorite subject is

_____.

It is my favorite because

_____.

My best friend is

_____.

My favorite food is

_____.

The food I hate the most is

_____.

My favorite movie/television show is

_____.

My favorite actor/singer is

_____.

My favorite book is

_____.

The things I like to do for fun are

_____.

Sports I play:

_____.

My foster parents' names are _____. I think

they are _____ (nice, fun, don't know yet).

I have _____ foster brothers and foster sisters. Their names are

_____.

Tell All

(Write as much as you can. If you don't know how you feel, you can

circle the emotions listed.)

This is my first day in foster care. I feel:

SCARED   SAD

LONELY   HAPPY   EXCITED

MAD   WEIRD

I feel this way because: _____

_____

_____

Draw a picture of the outside of your foster home or your bedroom.

Chapter 2

"When Do I Get to See My Parents?"

Visiting Day

It's understandable that you miss your parents and want to see them right away.

Visits are #1 at Child Welfare, but sometimes it can feel like they aren't happening fast enough. It can seem that way because there are all kinds of people involved with your visit other than you and your parents.

How is that possible?

Imagine you are at a school play. The actors on the stage keep you entertained with their clever lines, fancy dance steps, and charming songs. But what you don't see is all the people backstage, shuffling around and getting everything ready for the next act.

Scheduling visits can sort of feel like a play. The people backstage, like your foster parents and your caseworker, are busy preparing the best possible visit for you.

Remember, you are important and your visits are too.

At first, visits are almost always at the Child Welfare office in special rooms with toys, puzzles, and books.

Why?

Safety, safety, safety!

You'll hear this word a lot while you're in foster care.

To be on the *safe* side, visits take place where other adults can watch and make sure you're okay.

Since many kids come to the Child Welfare office to visit their parents, visiting rooms are booked way in advance. Usually, these bookings go through either your case worker or a team of people called SOCIAL SERVICE ASSISTANTS. Social Service Assistants are like "booking managers" because they schedule the rooms and watch the visits.

Once your room is chosen, the assistant calls your foster parents and parents. If everyone can be at office at the same time, then a visit is scheduled.

Don't worry about how you'll get there. Your foster parents, caseworker, or assistant will make sure you arrive on time.

Visits are supposed to be a fun and happy time for both your parents and you. You can play games, read books, or talk during your special time together.

Kids feel many things about visits. Some feel excited, sad, or unhappy about visiting their parents. Whatever you're feeling, it is okay. You're allowed to feel different things, too.

What if I don't get to visit my parents?

If you're not having visits right now, it's never, *ever* because of you.

When kids don't have visits with their parents, it's for very good reasons. Some of the reasons could be a parent being away, in jail, or sick, but another reason might be safety. If there is a concern that children could get hurt during a visit, then no one will take any chances.

Foster care is all about you and making sure you're safe.

Chapter 2 Workbook

Visits are a fun and happy time, so enjoy them. Make sure you play, laugh, and talk with your parent or parents. Then, write about some of the things you did.

My first visit with my parent(s) was (date): _____.

Some of the things we did:

1. _____

2. _____

3. _____

Some of the things we talked about:

1. _____

2. _____

3. _____

On a scale of one to ten, with ten being the best, rank your

visit:_____.

How could your visit been better? Explain. (For example, *I would have liked more toys* or *I would have liked to play a board game*.)

Our visits are scheduled for (day of the week): _____.

At our next visit, I would like to:

1. _____

2. _____

3. _____

Tell All

How did you feel about your visit?

HAPPY   SAD

EXCITED   BORED   MAD

SCARED   WEIRD

Why did you feel this way? _____

_____

_____

Paste a photo or draw a picture of you and your parent(s) at your visit.

Chapter 3

"What About My Brothers or Sisters?"

Brothers and Sisters Are Important, Too!

Brothers and sisters don't always go to the same foster home.

But why?

Sometimes there is not enough room in one home.

This can be a little like playing musical chairs. The music starts to play and you go 'round and 'round until the music stops. You scramble for a seat, but someone else grabs it first.

Foster homes can sometimes seem like musical chairs because other kids who entered foster care before you are already in the home. Just like there aren't enough chairs in the game, there aren't enough beds in the home for all of you. You and your brothers and sisters all deserve a bed and a place to put your clothes and special things.

What if I'm separated from my brothers and sisters?

The special bonds you have with your brothers and sisters will remain strong. Every Child Welfare agency is committed to keeping those loving, giving, sharing, and (sometimes) bickering ties in one piece. And, usually, this is through visits.

Like how?

Foster parents can call up other foster parents and plan a time for your siblings and you to get together. This may be at the park or the local pizza place. Another way you will get visits with your brothers and sisters is at the Child Welfare office. You can also ask your foster parents if you can call your brothers and sisters at their foster home.

Sometimes brothers and sisters won't see each other. Like with parents, visits with brothers and sisters will not be scheduled if there's a safety concern and somebody might get hurt. Another reason might be that your brother or sister tries to get you to do bad things, like run away or harm others.

Will I ever get to live with my brothers or sisters again?

It's a goal at Child Welfare to keep siblings together. As soon as a foster home has enough openings to take you and your brothers and sisters, your foster parents and caseworker will work to bring you all together (as long as there are no safety concerns).

Chapter 3 Workbook

You can answer questions about your *foster* brothers and *foster* sisters if you don't have any siblings.

I have _____ brothers and sisters.

Their names and ages are

_____.

Their birthdays are

_____.

Are they older or younger than you?

_____.

Are any of your siblings in school? What grade?

_____.

Do you know your brothers' and sisters' favorite colors/food/games?

_____

_____

Do any of your siblings play sports?

_____.

What do you like best about your brothers and sisters?

1. _____

2. _____

3. _____

Today, (date) _____, I had a visit with my siblings.

Some of the things we talked about:

1. _____

2. _____

3. _____

On a scale of one to ten, with ten being the best, rank your

visit:_____

How could your visit have been better? (For example, *I would have rather gone swimming* or *I would have played more games.*)

_____

Our next visit is (date) _____. At our next visit, we

would like to: _____.

Tell All

How did you feel about your visit?

HAPPY   SAD

EXCITED   BORED   ANGRY

SCARED   WEIRD

Why did you feel this way? _____

_____

_____

Paste a photo or draw a picture of you and your siblings at your visit.

Chapter 4

"Can't I Live with Grandma?"

Living with Relatives

Living with family seems simple enough, but your caseworker and foster parents keep talking about CERTIFICATION. What is that? And what does that long word have to do with you?

Certification is something Child Welfare does that gives "two thumbs up" to your grandma, grandpa, aunt, uncle, or any other relative before you're allowed to live in their home.

But I go to grandma's house all the time...

It's like when you want to spend the night at a friend's house and your parents say, "I need to talk to their parents first." Certification is almost the same thing. Child Welfare doesn't want just *anybody* taking care of you, so they need to talk to your relatives first.

Even though you may know your grandma, grandpa, aunt, and uncle better than anyone, they still have to go through the certification process with Child Welfare.

Certification involves background checks (to make sure they haven't done anything really bad), home visits (to see if there's plenty of room for you), and reference checks (to find out what others have to say about them).

This way, Child Welfare gets to know them too.

The good news is that nearly anyone you know can go through certification—even people who aren't your relatives. If family friends (people you've known your whole life) would like you to live with them, then they can be certified too.

How long does certification take?

The process can take anywhere from 24 hours to a month.

It can take a long time if there are problems or bumps in the road. For instance, your relatives will not be certified if they have hurt kids or other adults in the past, or if their home is unsafe. If there is even a slight chance that you might get hurt in your relative's home, then Child Welfare won't let you live there.

What then?

If your relatives or family friends can't be certified, your caseworker will keep looking for other relatives or family friends, even if they live in another state or country. If that's too far away for you, then make sure to tell your caseworker right away.

Chapter 4 Workbook

Do you have any relatives or family friends you want to live with?

1. _____

2. _____

3. _____

Are any of your family members or friends trying to get certified? Who?

1. _____

2. _____

3. _____

On (date) _____, my caseworker referred my relative or family friend for certification.

Is this person:

FUN	STRICT	KIND
SMART	A GOOD LISTENER	FRIENDLY

Do you know him/her: (Circle One)

      Really well   Somewhat well   Not at all

I went to go live with my certified relative or family friend on (date)

_____.

My new phone number and address is

_____.

The school I'm going to attend is

_____.

Some of the fun things we do at home:

_____.

Some of the new rules:

_____.

Are there any pets?

_____.

Tell All

How do you feel about living with your certified relative or family friend?

SCARED   SAD

LONELY   HAPPY   EXCITED

MAD   WEIRD

I feel this way because: _____

_____

_____

Paste a photo or draw a picture of you and your certified relative or family friend.

Part II

How Did It Happen?

One moment, everything was the same.

The next, your whole world changed.

Strangers came to your home or school. They spoke to your parents. They spoke to you. And then you left with people you'd just met.

Talk about feeling like you're in the middle of a storm!

How did it happen so fast?

Why did these people even come?

It's time to find out.

Chapter 5

"How Did They Know My Name?"

The Screener and the Report

Child Welfare workers show up at your school. They show up at your house. As a matter of fact, they can show up wherever you might be. How do they know where to find you? Not only that, but how do they seem to know everything about you, like your name and your birthday? Is it magic? Do they have special powers? Nope, it's none of that. The truth is that someone else tells them.

Say what?

Adults call the CHILD ABUSE HOTLINE when they have concerns that children are not safe. Callers can be anyone: babysitters, family members, or other parents. Some people are even MANDATORY REPORTERS like teachers, coaches, police officers, and doctors. It's *mandatory* for them because they *have* to report it.

They can get in big trouble if they know kids are unsafe and don't take action.

Grown-ups want to make sure kids are okay. Since it's so important for adults to call when they are worried, the hotline keeps their names top secret so that people don't get mad at them.

Who takes this information about me?

The people who get the Child Welfare process started are called SCREENERS.

Like telephone operators, screeners stay by the phones all day and take reports about kids in your town and city. When a call comes in to the hotline, they gather as much information as they can from the person making the call.

Screeners want to know all about you—it's their job.

Screeners want to know your name, your age, your address, your parents' names, and the names of your brothers and sisters (if you have any). If the person calling doesn't know, then screeners sometimes call your school to find out.

But that's not all.

Screeners also listen to the caller's concerns about you and ask questions, like how are you being treated? Do you have plenty of food to eat? Is your home safe?

That is the most important part of their job.

Every day, the Child Abuse Hotline receives hundreds of calls, but only a supervisor (the screener's boss) can give the okay to tell a caseworker to investigate.

A supervisor won't send a caseworker if there are no safety concerns in the report. For example, it's not okay to call if you don't like what's for dinner, you can't spend the night at a friend's house, or you are grounded.

But if things are happening in your home that could really hurt you physically (your body), mentally (your mind), or emotionally (your feelings), then a supervisor will send a caseworker right away!

Everyone deserves to be safe, especially you.

Chapter 5 Workbook

My screener's name is

_____.

The report about me came in to the hotline on (date)

_____.

The report said:

1. _____

2. _____

3. _____

I think the report is: True   Not true   A little true

(Why? or Why not?) _____

_____

The supervisor's safety concerns were:

1. _____

2. _____

3. _____

Tell All

The report made me feel:

MAD   EMBARRASSED

SAD   WORRIED   HAPPY

THANKFUL   GLAD

Why did you feel this way? _____

_____

_____

_____

_____

_____

_____

_____

Ask your screener to write something about you here:

_____

_____

_____

_____

_____

_____

_____

_____

_____

_____

_____

Chapter 6

"Why Are They Worried About My Safety?"

The Intake Worker and the Assessment

You were sitting at home and everything was pretty much the same. Then you heard a knock on the door and strangers came inside. They said they were from Child Welfare and they wanted to talk about safety. Questions seemed to fly right at you and, before you knew it, the people from Child Welfare said you were going with them.

Why? Why? Why?

The Child Welfare caseworkers had placed you in PROTECTIVE CUSTODY.

Kids are placed in protective custody when there is a chance something bad might happen if they stay with their parents. Only Child Welfare caseworkers and police officers can place children in protective custody.

49

But, how could you know something would happen to me?

It's almost like figuring out a mystery. Was it Professor Plum in the library? Or maybe it was Mrs. Peacock in the study? It's impossible to tell without looking at the clues.

Like a mystery, there are clues that something might happen or has happened to you.

CHILD ABUSE means somebody hurt your body. A caseworker or police officer might get clues that you've been abused if you have large bruises, broken bones, or bad burns.

CHILD NEGLECT is when you're not getting the things you need. As with child abuse, a caseworker or police officer might suspect you're being neglected if you're home alone a lot, your parents use drugs, or you don't have enough food to eat.

No child should ever be abused or neglected.

Child Welfare caseworkers and police officers take child abuse and neglect very seriously. If a report comes in to the Child Abuse Hotline that you may be getting hurt, then Child Welfare caseworkers and police officers will come to your home or school to talk about SAFETY.

You're safe when you *know* nothing will hurt you and you're being taken care of.

If you don't *know* you're safe, then tell an adult (like your teacher). Kids can't protect or care for themselves. They need grown-ups to do that for them!

Then what?

If there are worries about your safety, then you will meet a police officer or an INTAKE CASEWORKER. An intake caseworker investigates child abuse and child neglect.

Intake caseworkers will come to your school or your home to talk and ask questions. If they think you are unsafe, then the caseworker may place you into protective custody to make sure you'll be okay.

Chapter 6 Workbook

The intake caseworker came to my home or school on (date):

_____.

My intake caseworker's name is

_____.

My intake caseworker's phone number is

_____.

The caseworker's supervisor's name is

_____.

After talking to my intake caseworker, I was taken into protective

custody because:

1. _____

2. _____

3. _____

I think the reason(s) were: Good   Bad   Okay

Protective custody makes me feel:

MAD   BETTER

HAPPY   SAD   WEIRD

WORRIED   SO-SO

Why do you feel this way?

Tell All

What happened the day the caseworkers showed up at your home or school? _____

_____

_____

If I had my way, I would have: _____

_____

_____

I feel this way because: _____

_____

_____

Paste your intake caseworker's business card

Ask your intake caseworker to write something about you.

_____

_____

_____

_____

_____

Chapter 7

"Why Do My Parents Have To Go To Court?" From Judges to Attorneys and Everyone in Between

The COURTROOM is a place where many people go to talk about you.

What's it like?

Have you ever been to the circus? You disappear under the big top and you see the ringleader in the center ring. He raises his cane and yells, "Ladies and gentlemen, children of all ages..." You know the circus is about to start because the ringleader runs the show, right?

JUDGES are like ringleaders because they run the courtroom. They say when things start and when they stop. Instead of wearing top hats and red jackets, judges wear black robes and sit at tall desks. Judges get to say who can and cannot talk in court, and they can make people do things—even if they don't want to.

Even though judges are the ringleaders, you're still the star of the show.

Judges want to know all about you—how you are doing, what you need, how your parents are taking care of you, and what your parents are doing to take *better* care of you.

Judges can't know all these things when they haven't actually met you, so like the ringleader, they call in the performers: the ATTORNEYS. Instead of walking on tightropes or juggling, attorneys wear suits and talk to judges. Your attorney's job is to be the spokesman and make sure you get what you need.

I get an attorney?

Depending on your state, you will have an attorney, a COURT APPOINTED SPECIAL ADVOCATE (CASA), or a GUARDIAN AD LITEM (child's advocate).

Your attorney, CASA, or guardian ad litem will meet with you to find out everything about you. He or she will ask if you're happy at your foster home or if you're getting visits with your parents and siblings.

Because your attorney, CASA, or guardian ad litem talks for you in court, you should tell him/her everything you want the judge to know.

Your parent or parents will also get an attorney because of the PETITION. A petition is a report given to judges that says how parents made things unsafe at home. It might say the home was too dirty or someone was using drugs.

Things written on the petition may not always be right, so attorneys talk to judges for parents. If the parents agree that the petition is true, then attorneys tell the judges what parents are doing to make things better.

Judge, judge, judge. What gives?

Judges make all the final decisions about you. They decide if you stay with your foster parents or return home to your parents. When judges make those decisions, they want to do what's best, even if it doesn't feel that way sometimes.

Judges are always on your side, and they make sure *everyone* is working hard for you.

Chapter 7 Workbook

My judge's name is

_____.

My attorney, CASA, or guardian ad litem's name is

_____.

His/her phone number is

_____.

Some of the things my attorney, CASA, or Guardian Ad Litem and I

talk about: (Circle)

MY PARENTS   SCHOOL   MY FOSTER PARENTS

MY BROTHERS AND SISTERS   ME   OTHER THINGS

My attorney, CASA, or guardian ad litem has told the judge:

1. _____

2. _____

3. _____

My attorney, CASA, or guardian ad litem said that the judge wants:

1. _____

2. _____

3. _____

Tell All

What do you think of your attorney, CASA, or guardian ad litem?

SMART   FUNNY   NICE

CARING   QUIET   A GOOD LISTENER

INTERESTED IN WHAT I HAVE TO SAY

I think my attorney, CASA, or guardian ad litem is doing a:

GOOD JOB   BAD JOB   SO-SO JOB

I feel this way because: _____

_____

_____

What I'd like my attorney, CASA, or guardian ad litem to change for me:

1. _____

2. _____

3. _____

Paste your attorney, CASA, or guardian ad litem's card.

Paste a picture or draw a picture of your judge, attorney, CASA, or guardian ad litem.

Part III

What's Going to Happen?

You've learned a lot about why you entered foster care and what you can expect while in foster care.

What happens now?

The future can mean a hundred different things and a thousand different outcomes.

What's going on with your parents?

How long will you stay in foster care?

When will you go home?

These tough questions can have even tougher answers.

Chapter 8

"How Long Do I Have to Live Here?"

You and the Permanency Caseworker

You will only be in foster care until your home is safe enough for you to return.

How long will that be?

It depends on your parents and your PERMANENCY CASEWORKER. Permanency caseworkers are involved throughout your entire case, which means you'll be seeing them a lot.

Permanency caseworkers do two things. First, they make sure that parents are learning better ways to take care of their kids. Second, they work to get kids the things they need while in foster care.

Even though permanency caseworkers work a lot with moms and dads, they help kids too. Permanency caseworkers make sure that kids are going to school, visiting the doctor, seeing the dentist, and getting counseling.

Permanency caseworkers make hard decisions about whether or not it's okay for kids to return home to their parents. They want kids to be happy, but their most important job is to make sure kids are safe. They won't recommend that kids return home until they know for sure.

What am I supposed to do in the meantime?

You should do what you normally do, like go to school, play sports, and hang out with friends. If you need some more ideas, ask your permanency caseworker to get you involved in karate, gymnastics, or dance classes.

Your permanency caseworker understands that foster care is not easy, so he or she will do everything possible to make it a better experience.

Did you know you can also help your caseworker?

How?

You can help by telling your caseworker what you need, how you're feeling, and what you think your parents need to keep you safe.

Foster care is all about you. It's your show!

Chapter 8 Workbook

My permanency caseworker's name is

_____.

His/her phone number is

_____.

His/her supervisor's name is

_____.

I usually see my permanency caseworker _____ times per month.

Some of the things my permanency caseworker and I do:

1. _____

2. _____

3. _____

On a scale of one to ten, with ten being the best, our visits are a

_____.

Some of the things that my permanency caseworker is doing for me:

1. _____

2. _____

3. _____

Tell All

Some of the things I like about my permanency caseworker:

1. _____

2. _____

3. _____

I wish my permanency caseworker would:

1. _____

2. _____

3. _____

Some of the things I've talked about with my permanency

caseworker:

1. _____

2. _____

3. _____

Paste your permanency caseworker's business card.

Ask your permanency caseworker to write something about you.

_____

_____

_____

_____

_____

Chapter 9

"What's Happening with My Parents While I'm Away?"

Your Parents and Your Caseworker

You've been busy being a kid: doing your homework, going to the movies, getting to know your foster brothers and sisters, and hanging out at the mall.

What about your parents? What have they been doing?

They've been as busy as you!

Doing what?

Your parents have been working on a plan to make sure they can take better care of you. Child Welfare and the courts call this the PRIMARY PLAN, which is sort of a Plan A.

Plan A?

Foster care is okay for now, but what about your future? You need a permanent home, but that can't be any home. Your home must be safe, and a place where you're happy and have everything you need (like food and clothes).

Plan A will make sure you get it.

How does Plan A work?

Let's pretend you're at boot camp. You wake up at 5 a.m., make your bed, put on your uniform, run five miles, do push-ups, climb ropes, and so on. Why would you do all that? The answer: You're learning to be a soldier.

Your parents are learning to take good care of you.

Your parents may go to parenting classes, counseling, and drug and alcohol treatment. Or they may do other things, like find a safe home or a good job. Plan A includes all the things your parents must do to make your home safe.

Are you saying that when my parents are done, I can go back home?

The main goal is to return you home to your parents. If they have done everything to assure you'll be safe and can show they'll make sure you *stay* safe, then it will be time to go home.

Going home is a big decision made by many people, including your permanency caseworker, the judge, your attorney, your parents, and you.

Chapter 9 Workbook

Plan A is for me to return home.

I think a safe home has:

1. _____

2. _____

3. _____

Some of the things my parents are doing right now to make sure I'm

safe:

1. _____

2. _____

3. _____

My parents think these are important because:

1. _____

2. _____

3. _____

My permanency caseworker thinks these are important because:

1. _____

2. _____

3. _____

I think the things my parents are doing: Will help   Won't help

(Why? Why not?)

I would like to see my parents do the following:

1. _____

2. _____

3. _____

Tell All

If I were the caseworker, my plan for my parents would be:

_____

_____

_____

_____

I would want them to do these things because:

_____

_____

_____

Draw a picture of what you'd like your home to look like.

Chapter 10

"What Happens If I Never Get to Go Home?"

Adoption to Guardianship

Foster care is not forever. You will be going home, but not always the one you expected.

THE ADOPTIONS AND SAFE FAMILIES ACT (ASFA) says that kids shouldn't be in foster care for years and years.

All kids need permanent homes. You are no different.

ASFA sets a due date for when your parents need to complete Plan A. This way, you don't always hear "soon," "I don't know," and "maybe" about going home.

What happens if my parents don't complete Plan A?

In addition to Plan A, there is also Plan B, or the CONCURRENT PLAN. "Concurrent" means that Plan B is happening at the same time as Plan A.

How?

Picture a car race.

A red sports car (Plan A) and a blue sports car (Plan B) fire up their engines at the starting line. The green light flashes and both cars tear out of the gate, leaving waves of smoke.

Will the blue car win or the red one?

You're on the edge of your seat as you watch the cars whip around the final turn and fly down the track. Suddenly, the red car sputters and slows down. The blue sports car jumps ahead, tearing across the finish line and winning the race.

Like in a car race, it's hard to predict what will happen, which is why there are always two plans.

Okay, okay, I get it. What's Plan B all about?

You may find this hard to believe, but you're not going to be a kid forever. While you are, you will need a safe, permanent, and healthy place to live. If your parents can't provide that for you, that doesn't mean you can't have it at all.

You can! You deserve it! That's what "Plan B" is all about.

You can still have a safe, healthy, and permanent home with other grown-ups through ADOPTION or GUARDIANSHIP.

Adoption means you become part of another family. You become a new brother or sister, daughter or son. In most cases, your last name changes to your new family's last name. Even though everyone is *born* into a family, happy and safe families are *created* with adoption.

Guardianship works a little differently from adoption.

Imagine that your Aunt Kathy wanted to be your guardian. With adoption, Aunt Kathy wouldn't be your aunt, but more like your mom. With guardianship, Aunt Kathy will still be Aunt Kathy, but she will take care of you from now on and make sure you're safe. Just like with adoption, you'll live at your guardian's house, but you'll probably keep your last name.

If you're adopted or placed in a guardianship, this doesn't mean you can't ever see your parents again. Most times, your adoptive parents or guardians will make sure you still have a relationship with your birth parents.

The great thing about Plan B is that you can be adopted or placed in a guardianship with one of your relatives, or even with your foster parents.

Chapter 10 Workbook

On what date did you and your caseworker start working on Plan B?

_____

My Plan B will be: GUARDIANSHIP   or   ADOPTION

       I like this plan   I don't like this plan

Why or why not?

_____

_____

_____

Who would you like to live with until you grow up? Explain why.

1. _____

2. _____

3. _____

What kind of family would you like to have while you grow up?

(For example: a family with two parents or one parent, animals or no animals, in the city or in the country?)

1. _____

2. _____

3. _____

What do you like most about Plan B?

1. _____

2. _____

3. _____

What do you dislike most about Plan B?

1. _____

2. _____

3. _____

Tell All

How do you feel about living with grown-ups other than your parents until you grow up?

HAPPY   SAD   EXCITED

MAD   SCARED

I feel this way because: _____

_____

_____

When I grow up, I want to be: _____

_____

_____

What's the most important thing you learned about yourself in foster

care? _____

_____

_____

If you could change one thing about foster care, what would it be?

_____

_____

_____

Draw or paste a photo of you and your guardians or adoptive parents.

A Special Letter from Your Caseworker

_____

_____

_____

_____

_____

_____

_____

_____

_____

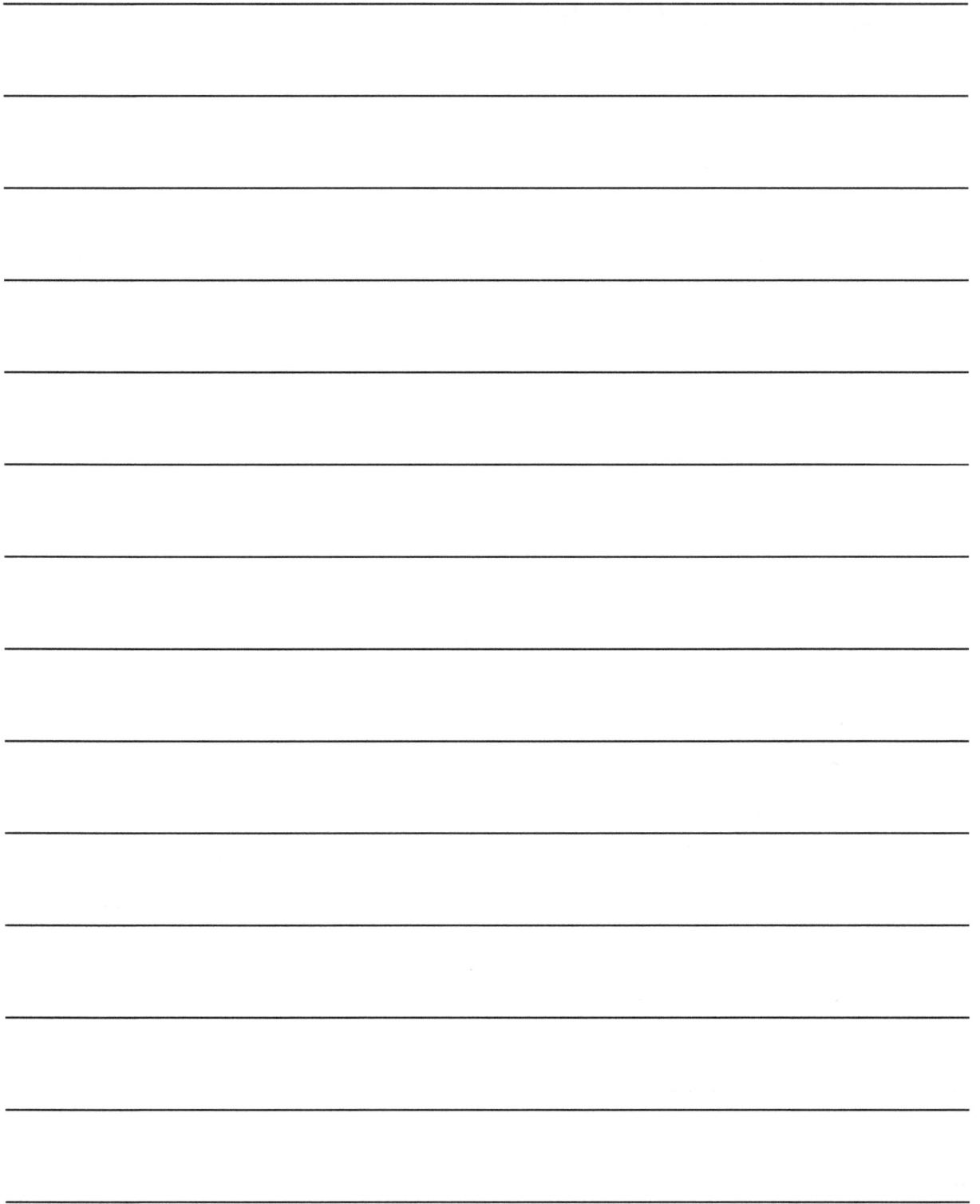

A Special Letter from Your Biological Parents

_____

_____

_____

_____

_____

_____

_____

_____

_____

_____

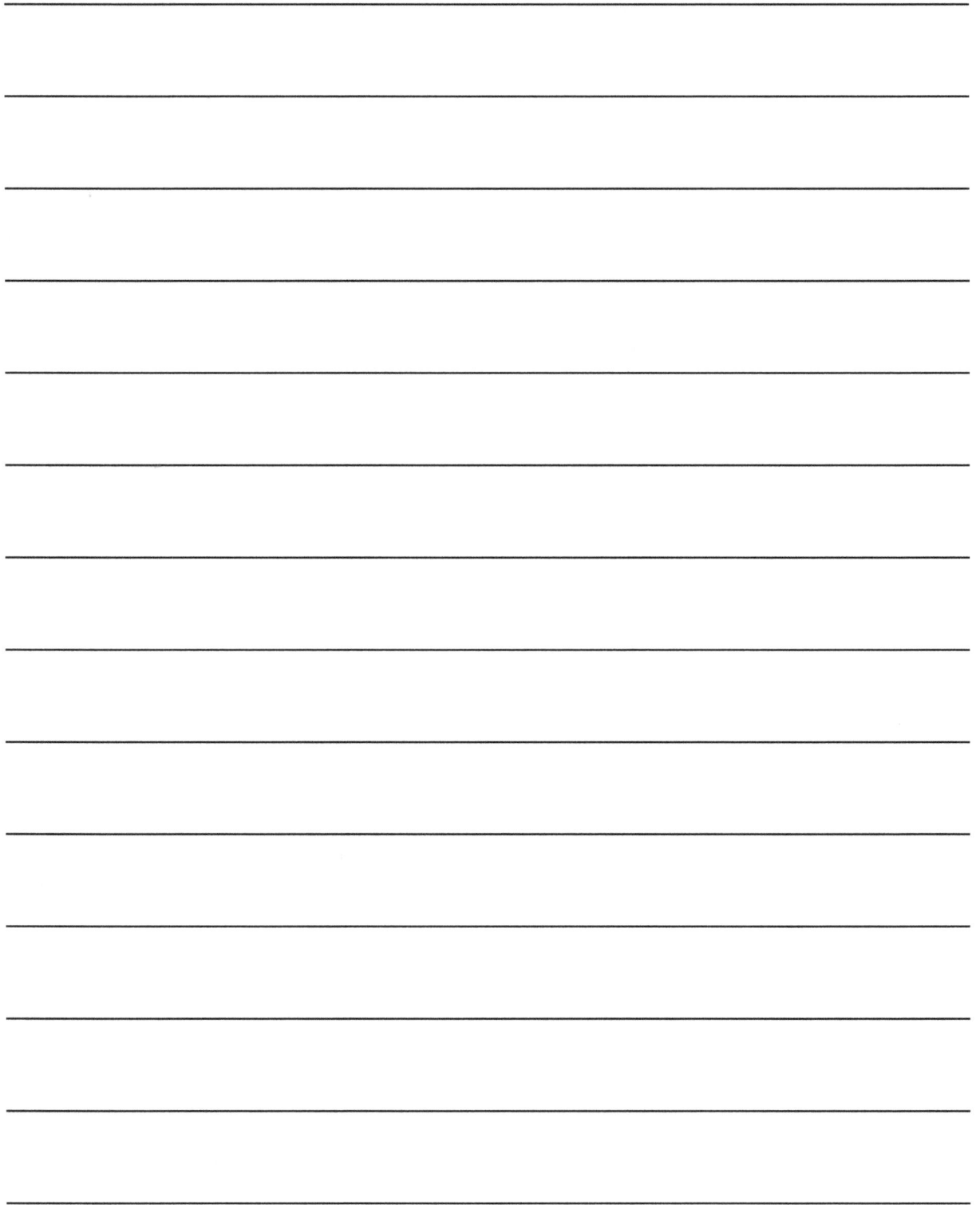

A Special Letter from Your

Adoptive Parents/Guardians

_____

_____

_____

_____

_____

_____

_____

_____

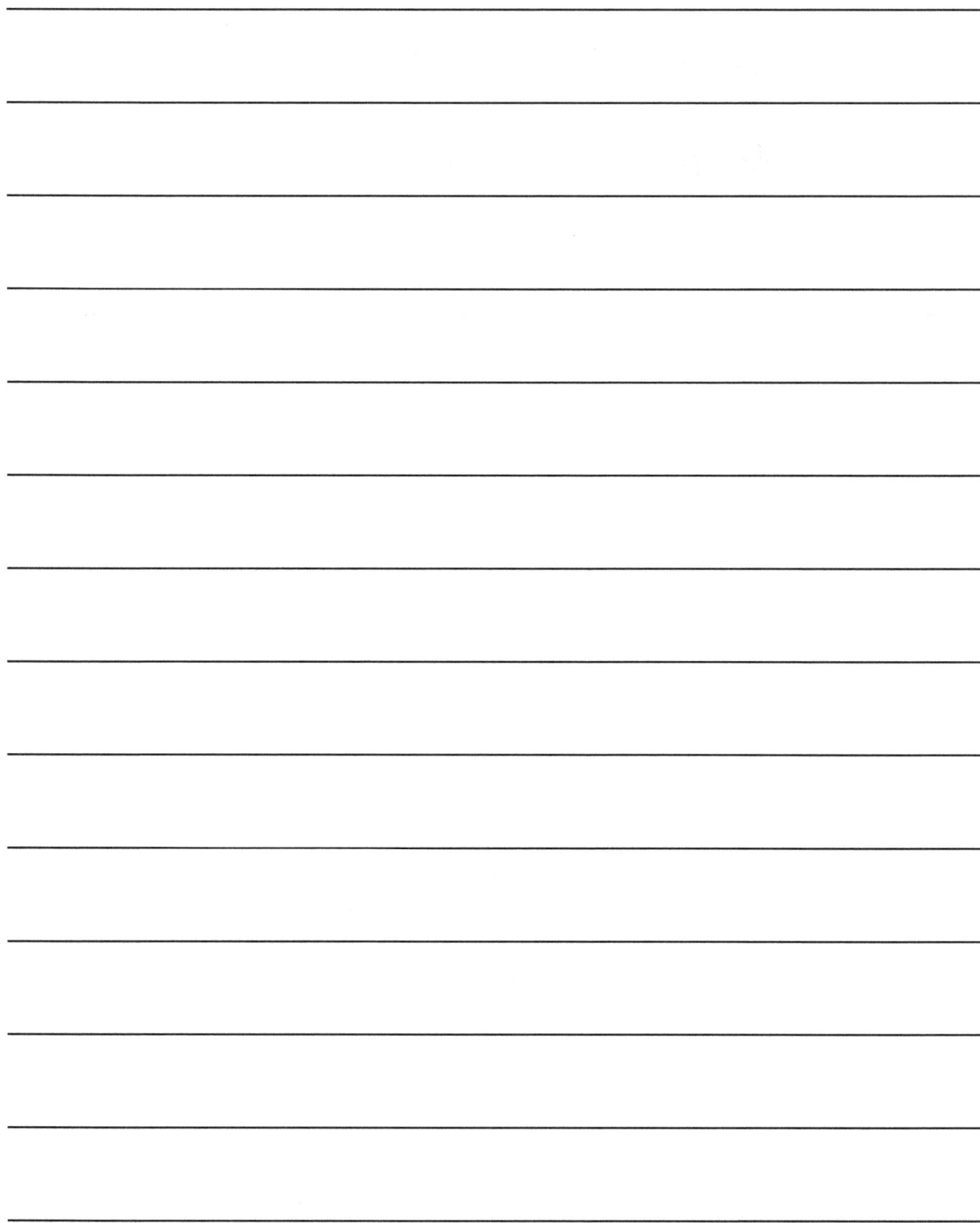

Glossary of Terms

Adoption: A legal process that makes children permanent members of another family

Adoptions and Safe Families Act (ASFA): A law that gives parents a deadline (15-22 months) for completing services before the concurrent plan takes effect

Attorney: A member of the court who speaks to the judge for his or her client

Certification: A process that allows relatives and family friends to become foster parents

Child Abuse: Physical, sexual, mental, and/or emotional abuse of a child

Child Abuse Hotline: A telephone service adults can call to report suspected child abuse and/or child neglect

Child Neglect: A type of abuse that deprives a child of basic needs like food, clothing, housing, and medical care

Child Welfare Intake Caseworker: A worker who investigates reports of child abuse and/or child neglect

Child Welfare Permanency Caseworker: A worker who provides services to parents and children who have open cases with Child Welfare

Concurrent Plan (Plan B): A plan for children to have permanent homes even if they cannot return to their parents

Court-Appointed Special Advocate (CASA): An adult who volunteers to work with children in foster care to support, guide, and go to court on their behalf

Courtroom: A room where legal issues are brought before a judge

Foster Home: A home where children live when it's not safe for them to be with their parents

Foster Parents: Adults who care for children when it's not safe for them to be with their parents

Guardian Ad Litem: An adult who makes legal decisions for children

Guardianship: A legal process that allows other adults to provide care for children until they turn 18

Judge: A person who makes all the final decisions in court and can order parents to complete services and tasks

Mandatory Reporter: A person who works with children on an everyday basis (such as a teacher, coach, or counselor) and is required to report suspected child abuse and/or neglect

Petition: A legal document that outlines how parents made their children unsafe

Primary Plan (Plan A): A plan for children to return home to their parents

Protective Custody: An action that police officers and caseworkers take when children are unsafe and need protection

Safety: A state of being without serious risk or threat of harm

Screener: A worker who answers calls to the Child Abuse Hotline and takes reports of child abuse and/or child neglect

Social Service Assistants: Workers who assist caseworkers and children in foster care with scheduling, arranging, and monitoring visits

www.ingramcontent.com/pod-product-compliance
Lightning Source LLC
Chambersburg PA
CBHW082332110426
42744CB00038B/1948